The Suits & Geeks Trap

Get your commercial and technical
people to work with you,
not against each other

Andy Bass, Ph.D

CONTENTS

PRAISE FOR THE SUITS & GEEKS TRAP

The Suits & Geeks Trap is a great guide for leaders navigating the challenge of bringing commercial and technical people together. It's authentic, concise and to the point, providing practical steps to transform differences into strengths.
Katherine Lamb, Transformation Director, Kraken Technology (Octopus Energy Group)

The Suits & Geeks Trap is a refreshing, entertaining read that gets straight to the point. It doesn't claim to be the panacea for business, but offers quick, actionable ideas that make you stop and think—something Andy excels at!
David J Pritchett,Co-founder, Viah Beauty, and former President, Rieke Packaging Systems

Andy playfully caricatures 'Suits' & the 'Geeks' to help us see a bigger picture. He shows us how to rise above stereotypes and fixed mindsets to get the best from people, ideas and technology.
Hanifa Shah, Pro-Vice Chancellor for STEAM and Executive Dean, Computing, Engineering and the Built Environment, Birmingham City University

The Suits & Geeks Trap is a great mirror for any business leader caught between commercial and technical teams. If you want to reduce frustration and align your teams to produce results, this book will be an excellent guide.
Paul Heldens, Director of Business Development, Roca Group

I've seen the Suit v Geek drama. It's real. And it's hard to think of a bigger (and more annoying) anchor on growth. That's why this book is necessary – to give practical solutions so you can turn your strategic ambition into reality.
Alex Smith, Author of "No Bulls*t Strategy"

Andy's ideas have helped us hugely during a period of intense digitally-driven growth. The Suits & Geeks Trap is a fast and friendly guide to aligning tech and commercial teams. It highlights the need to understand distinct motivations and cautions against what he calls the Organisational Development Delusion. Essential for leaders in the digital growth era.
Jurga Žilinskienė MBE, Founder and CEO/CTO, Guildhawk

Every business leader with a technical team should read The Suits and Geeks Trap. Andy clearly identifies common issues that both 'Suits' and 'Geeks' will recognise. Full of practical advice – a masterpiece!
Martin Worner, Co-founder Confio GmbH, Co-author of "Work Remotely".

"IT is no longer just about keeping the lights on. AI and data analytics have put it at the top of the agenda for executives and the board. To meet the new demands, technical and commercial teams must find better ways to understand each other. The Suits & Geeks Trap is a clear, helpful read for anyone facing the challenge.
Jo Hodson, Head of IT Services, Birmingham Airport

Andy gives C-Suite executives the Rosetta Stone for getting 'business' people and techies to cooperate for the good of the business and its customers.
Sean Bacon CD, Conflict Management Advisor, former fractional COO of Langley Concrete Group and performance mindset coach to the Canadian Women's Olympic Gold Rowing Team.

Foreword, by Ian Constance

CEO, The Advanced Propulsion Centre (UK) and former Global Chief Engineer, Ford Motor Company

Across industries, the challenges we face are becoming more complex and interconnected. Accelerating technological changes, geopolitical pressures on supply chains and the global push for sustainable practices all demand a new kind of collaboration inside our companies. The market is moving fast, and it's clear that success will hinge on how well we bring together our commercial and technical minds.

Having experienced my fair share of both product design meetings and quarterly projection presentations, I've seen what happens when communication breaks down between these two camps. And let's be honest, it happens more often than we'd like. Both sides are under immense pressure, but they can seem like they're talking different languages. It's no wonder that frustrations arise, especially for leaders who need fast results.

The Suits & Geeks Trap tackles that head-on. It doesn't suggest a one-size-fits-all solution, nor does it imply that commercial people should try to be like engineers, or vice versa. Instead, it looks at how we can find a way through these challenges by respecting the different perspectives and motivations at play. In my own sector – automotive – we're used to designing and building with precision: each component must fit perfectly into the whole. The relationship between our technical and commercial teams is no different. It's about getting the right fit.

Engineers need to know they have the resources to develop reliable, efficient technologies. At the same time, commercial teams must secure those resources by communicating value to customers and investors.

The road is rarely smooth. This book offers practical strategies to get both sides working together, rather than butting heads over who's to blame when things go wrong.

What I like about Andy's book is its focus on being pragmatic. It steers away from abstract exercises that can feel disconnected from the day job. Instead, it dives into the nuts and bolts of collaboration. It looks at where things are already working well and how to leverage those successes to build more productive relationships in the workplace, not just a training room. This should appeal to leaders who can't afford to spend months in workshops or seminars while the market races ahead. We need solutions that work in real time.

The future will be more digital and must be more sustainable. The stakes couldn't be higher. The path forward will be challenging, requiring careful planning, investment, and, above all, collaboration between our technical and commercial minds. This book is an important resource for navigating that path. It helps you not just manage the tension between the 'Suits' and the 'Geeks,' but actually turn that tension into a driving force for innovation and growth.

So, as you dive into this book, think about the big picture. Think about the human value of the technologies you're all working to build. And remember: the real breakthroughs happen when we bring all talents to the table, speaking openly, honestly, and with a shared sense of purpose.

THE IDEA IN A NUTSHELL

Every great tech-heavy business has been built by commercially- and technologically-minded people working together. In fact, synergy between entrepreneurial business people and ingenious tech folk is arguably the force that's built the modern world: from iPhones to jet airliners, from MRI scanners to air conditioners, from skyscrapers to vacuum cleaners. The biggest tech-giants to the humblest mom-and-pop suppliers all depend on a balance between commercial and technical mindsets.

But the fact is that **commercial and technical people sometimes drive each other nuts**. They all too easily fall into the trap of stereotyping each other: "Suits are like this" & "Geeks are like that". Communication breaks down and the business suffers.

When managers don't listen to engineers, it can lead to product recalls, customer losses, shredded reputations, and even disasters. When engineers don't listen to commercial people, it can lead to missed opportunities and the failure of once-great businesses.

And of course, each side blames the other, while you act as referee and then try to explain to the board why competitors are racing ahead. You're caught in the Suits & Geeks trap.

Many attempts a consultant might recommend fail because they kid themselves that you can make one tribe think and act like the other. You try to make commercial teams understand the engineers and they get impatient with the jargon and the detail. You try to get engineers to be like marketers and you get eye-rolling, lip-service commitments and you drive their tinkering underground.

You might be tempted to try team-building, personality tests, project management software and business school courses. But while they all seem a good idea at the time – and they *might* plausibly be *part* of a solution – they never quite do the trick.

You're trying to solve the problem but what you really need to do is *dissolve* it.

That means stopping attempts to force or inadvertently manipulate square pegs into round holes, and finding the natural synergy that is always there, waiting to be re-established.

And that's the good news: We know that commercial people and engineers can collaborate magnificently: because that's what built the modern world. You've also probably experienced times when such collaboration happened in your own career. So it can happen again.

By the time you've read this book, you'll know what has to happen to get your commercial and technical people working *with you* rather than against each other.

THE IDEA IN PRACTICE

1. **Appeal to the wildly different mindsets of engineers and business managers.** Business people need technology to make money. Engineers need money to make technology.

2. **Don't try and change people's motivations.** You can't motivate people – they're already motivated. Appeal to what they're already interested in. Avoid their existing turn-offs.

3. **Stop pursuing 'solutions' that actually make things worse.** The tools consultants use can exacerbate the problem and tighten the trap, because they often make people feel pushed or patronised. And people are very creative in how they resist being pushed.

4. **Sort out your top team relationships.** Any Suit v Geek tensions on the leadership team will be reflected in 'proxy battles' around the rest of the organization.

5. **Don't make people sing 'Kumbaya'.** It's a guaranteed recipe for cynicism.

6. **Start with what works.** Turn exceptions into interventions. Where do your supposed 'Suits' and 'Geeks' work well together? Where do people act counter to the stereotype (it might be at work, it might be outside work. Either way it can be leverage). By the way, *Start With What Works* is the title of one of my books.

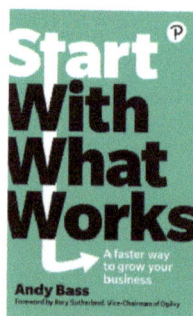

7. **Clarify incentives.** Are you inadvertently rewarding the behaviours that feed into Suit v. Geek games and therefore drive Doom Loops?

8. **Coach both sides on their individual effectiveness.** Both groups have legitimate challenges (e.g. perfectionism and procrastination among engineers and professionals, and bringing bad news and influencing across boundaries for business development). There's no substitute for interactive help from the right kind of coaches.

9. **Make sure you're not enabling destructive behaviour.** If you reward or promote people who like to play stupid Suits versus Geeks games, you send a far more powerful signal than any workshop or speech at an all-hands meeting about stopping the games.

10. **Improve relationships by working together on substantive tasks rather than relying on workshops.** Workshops – unless properly embedded – always run the risk of being forgotten as soon as people get back to their inbox. Keep it real.

If you're a leader who feels like your organization is caught in a trap, this is your escape plan.

These and other measures, explained in more detail below, will get your commercial and technical people to stop driving each other nuts so that they can get on with delivering results.

And then they won't be driving *you* nuts either!

ABOUT ME:
A GEEK WHO LEARNED TO WEAR A SUIT

Suit?

Geek?

Why listen to me? I'm a geek who put on a suit and learned to pass undetected – most of the time – in the C-suite. I speak both languages. I understand both mindsets, and I can translate between them. Here's how it happened:

- Shy kid disappeared into bedroom aged 13 and emerged at 17 able to play electric guitar. Only emerged when it was time to get the coveted driving licence.
- Summer jobs helping a mechanic fix cars.
- First degree in computer science and ergonomics, including placement at BT Research Labs, then a PhD in Software Engineering.
- Became a lecturer in Applied Psychology and Organization Studies at Aston Business School, researching and teaching Systems Thinking, AI and Change Management.
- Trained as a psychotherapist.
- Left the University to see if I could apply all this theory in the 'real world'.
- Got a savvy New York business mentor and learned to market my consulting services.

- Figured out how to network.
- Became a Board Director of Birmingham Forward (hanging out with lots of Suits from big law and accountancy firms).
- Started teaching Strategy to commercial clients of Aston Business Schools Exec Ed department include L'Oreal, BUPA, NSAN and RPC.
- Built consulting practice, working my way up to C-suite clients. Clients have included International Automotive Component Group, Rolls Royce, Deutsche Bank Operations International, Aon, DLA Piper, Rieke Packaging and The Advanced Propulsion Centre.
- Projects around the world.
- Four books on innovation and leadership (not counting this one) include one I taught on an Exec Ed programme at Oxford Saïd Business School.
- Have nice suits, but still fluent in Geek (visiting professor at Birmingham City University in Managerial Cybernetics and Consulting Practice).
- As well as being a professional speaker, like quite a few formerly shy kids, I'm a failed stand-up comedian.
- Still play the guitar (I played lead guitar in a Rush tribute band – geeky as rock music goes, but at the same time kind of cool, right?).

IT'S NOT ABOUT BEING RUDE TO ANYONE!

Are you sure?

When I was growing up, the word Geek was sometimes a bit of an insult. When I was doing my PhD in software engineering, I was on the wrong end of that insult myself a few times. And of course, the epithet 'Suit' has often been hurled around with a connotation of disrespect – I learned early on in my consulting career that if I was going to talk to the night shift, I'd be better to dress in a fleece and cargo pants.

These days, though, the world has changed, and now, for many people, Geeky is cool, and Suits are often thought glamorous.

I'm using both terms as widely-understood short-hands that are not to be taken too seriously. In fact, a big secret to managing the dynamics between the commercial and technical people is to recognise that while the stereotypes often have the ring of truth, none of us are really constrained by these definitions.

So, while we all know we're not supposed to stereotype, as a former Geek who learned to wear a Suit, I'm going to give myself permission...

And let's face it, both 'sides' are easy to caricature: you've got your engineers on one side, with their heads buried in technical drawings, dreaming in algorithms and speaking in equations. And then there's the MBA crowd, mistaking the spreadsheet for the business, acting like they've got the secret map to the treasure chest, and shouting, "We have to go from Good to Great!".

It's like two tribes with their own goals, their own secret handshakes, and totally different languages.

If you lead an organization that depends on these two tribes working well together, you know it can be tough. The business should be dramatically successful given all these clever people, but sometimes that's the very cause of the frustration.

And if you're really unlucky, you've got some organizational development consultant waffling on about shared values, personality types and starting with WHY! (There are a lot of ways that people try to get Suits and Geeks to play nicely together. And a lot of those ways are counter-productive).

So I'm not being rude to anyone, but I might tease them once in a while...

Well, I don't mind if he's rude about consultants!

Me either!

WHO ARE YOU?

You're a leader who is accountable for results, and those results depend on both commercial and technical performance.

Some of your direct reports would consider themselves primarily business people (salespeople, commercial teams, finance and legal, and so on). Others think of themselves as primarily technical experts (engineers, coders, designers, professionals, scientists).

You need all these people to work *with* you and not *against* each other (and frankly, you want less hassle and more, faster results).

You may have started your own career on either the technical or commercial sides, and then broadened out. A lot of my clients have been engineers or traditional professionals who moved into a business development role or did an MBA, and from there went into general management. Others have been entrepreneurs and sales people who got excited about the possibilities of technology. They often have a great grasp of human applications, if not the thorny details.

Like my clients, you get that a balance needs to be struck, but maybe your direct reports – e.g. head of engineering, sales director – are more tribal. Often when that's the case, the tensions that arise on your management team are then reflected down through the organization.

To help you get the most out of this book, consider the following:

1. When you started out in your career, were you more interested in business or in technical matters?

2. How did you develop a wider perspective? Was it because of certain experiences, mentors, etc?

3. Who among your direct reports "gets it" and who is still tribal?

4. Who among other key managers and influencers, gets it and who is still tribal?

5. What could your business achieve if commercial people and technical people played better together?

6. What issues do Suits & Geeks problems cause the business? What would happen if that improved?

7. What have you tried?

8. What one change – if you were able to accomplish it – would represent a great return on investment?

9. What *else* would be possible once you achieved that one change?

Part One

How Did We Get Here?

"Every great tech-based business has been built by incredible synergy between commercial and technical talent."

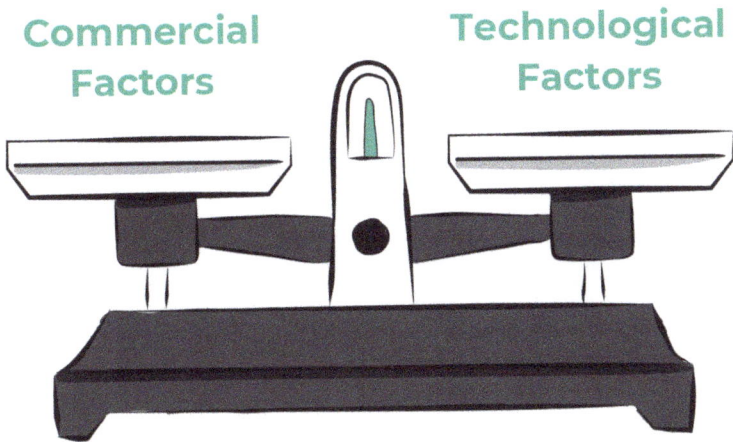

Great tech-based businesses are a balance of commercial and technological factors

THE BALANCING ACT THAT BUILT THE MODERN WORLD

The history of the modern world has been the product of a powerful synergy between two mindsets: the ingenuity of the engineers to apply scientific discoveries to practical problems, and the imagination of business people to make markets, orchestrate production & distribution, and figure out how to pay for it all.

Balancing those two mindsets has taken a special kind of leadership, whether from the earliest days of the Lunar Men at the start of the industrial revolution in England, through US pioneers such as Ford and Edison, to some of the great brands today.

Many companies could serve as examples, but here is a range:

- **Ford**. In at the beginning and still here today. Pioneer of mass production. Has reinvented itself successfully several times. The only major US auto maker that didn't take a government bailout during the 2008 financial crisis. True, it has also flirted with Suit-&-Geek type trouble at times, but has been resilient enough to survive and thrive as one of the world's oldest major companies still operating.

- It's a cliché but given the subject I can't fail to mention **Apple**. Famous for reinventing multiple industries, defining the way most of the world interacts with computers, creating the most successful consumer electronics products of all time (iPod in its day, and iPhone today), and regularly being in and out of top spot as the world's most valuable company. And a great *service* organization, too.

- **McLaren**. Winners of multiple Formula 1 championships. Has gone on to apply their capabilities to road-going supercars such as the hybrid McLaren P1. Beyond automotive, McLaren Applied Technologies uses their expertise to provides advanced engineering solutions in various industries, including healthcare, aerospace and energy.

- **Dyson**. For decades, people 'Hoovered' their carpets (even if their vacuum cleaner was made by someone else). Dyson reconceived the vacuum cleaner and now everyone copies them.

- **W L Gore and Associates**. Revolutionised the outdoor clothing industry with its invention of GORE-TEX®, a fabric that is both waterproof and breathable. Has made major advancements in medical technologies such as vascular grafts and surgical meshes. Makes cables good enough to be used on spacecraft. Consistently ranked as one of the best companies to work for, with high scores for innovation and employee satisfaction.

These and many other businesses I could have picked have found ways to create unique synergy between their commercial and technical talent.

But that doesn't mean getting those people to work together was easy! Because...

SUITS AND GEEKS
OFTEN DRIVE EACH OTHER CRAZY

It can be like the love-hate relationship between two very different siblings.

"As the leader, it's easy to end up as referee, while huge amounts of time are wasted delaying projects and slowing you down in the market."

_____

SUITS AND GEEKS HAVE DIFFERENT GOALS...

"Suits needs technology to make money.

Geeks need money to make technology."

And different ways of thinking...

How a Suit thinks about apples.   How a Geek thinks about apples.

SYNERGY OF THOSE GOALS DRIVES A GROWTH LOOP

While we're not supposed to stereotype, that doesn't mean there aren't differences. And when things are healthy, those differences are a good thing. Here's the biggest one:

Suits needs technology to make money.
Geeks need money to make technology.

It's worth taking a minute to really think about that. Depending on your own background, it could be the difference between confusion and clarity.

In the best case, this fundamental difference between commercial and technical people gives rise to a virtuous Growth Loop of value creation:

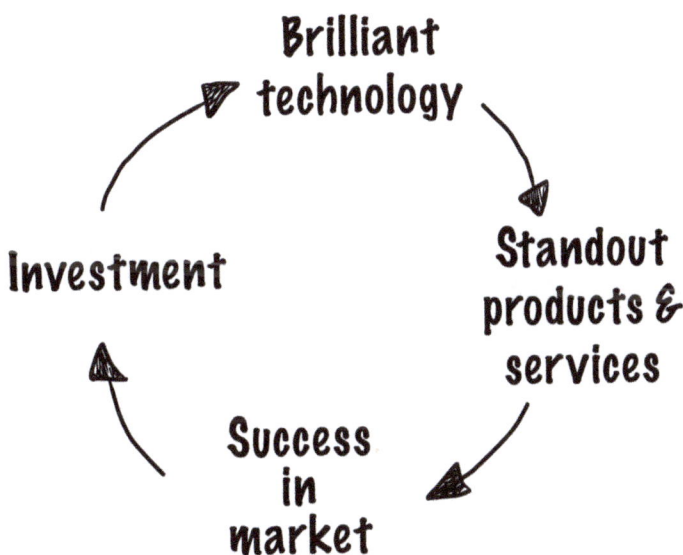

Brilliant technology → Standout products & services → Success in market → Investment → Brilliant technology

When it works, it's a beautiful thing.

BUT DIFFERENT GOALS AND MINDSETS CAN EASILY CLASH

The Suits vs Geeks Blame Game

THE BLAME GAME
DRIVES A DOOM LOOP

Relationships between Suits and Geeks are a bit like romantic relationships: romantic partners can create great joy for each other, or the same people can create great pain.

Similarly, when something goes wrong in the relationships between engineers and managers, it risks tipping the Growth Loop into a Doom loop.

And if you're the executive in charge of a business that's caught in a Doom Loop, it's frustrating as hell. The teams start bickering. They start blaming. They start playing games. They start spouting what I call "Tribal Wisdom." (more about that soon).

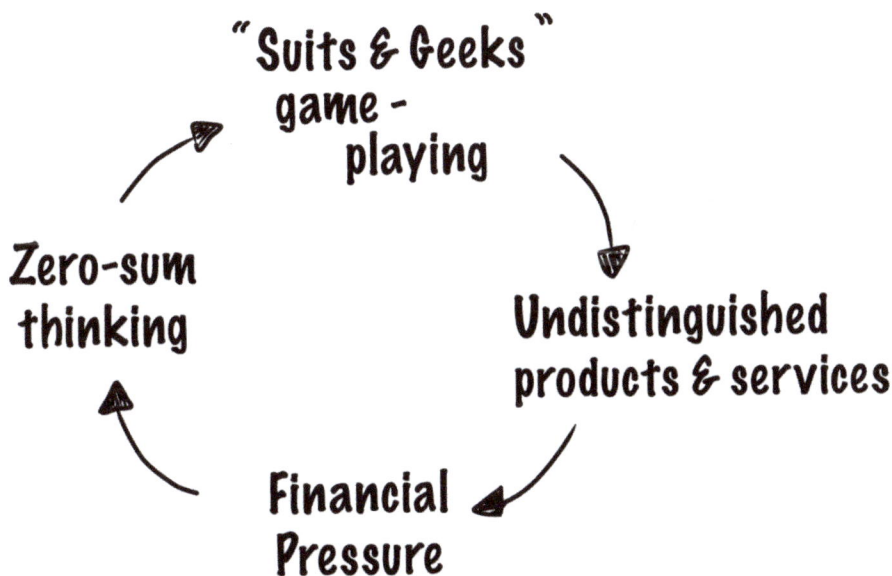

"Suits & Geeks"
game -
playing

Zero-sum
thinking

Undistinguished
products & services

Financial
Pressure

WHEN MANAGERS DON'T LISTEN TO 'THE GEEKS', IT CAN LEAD TO PRODUCT RECALLS, CUSTOMER LOSSES, SHREDDED REPUTATIONS, AND EVEN HEADLINE-GRABBING DISASTERS.

HOW THE SUITS FROM MCDONNELL DOUGLAS WRECKED BOEING

I have a friend who is comfortable thinking of himself as an Uber-Geek. He worked for decades in investment banking risk management, surrounded by a team of physics and statistics PhDs. He often bemoaned the inadequacies of people he saw as 'Suits' in the bank. He'd say: "In my experience, managers (meaning managers everywhere) are incompetent."

I *used* to have a sure-fire riposte: "Boeing." That would shut him up, at least for a few weeks.

But Boeing has been an extremely troubled company in recent years. It really is a salutary example of the mess Suits & Geeks can get into. First though, we should acknowledge that, as Lord King, former Chief Executive of British Airways once put it, "Boeing pretty much built the global airline industry" through its comprehensive range of brilliantly engineered long- and short-haul jet airliners.

But after their merger with McDonnell Douglas, Boeing's top-quality engineering-based culture was eroded by the Suits from McDonnell Douglas (there's a must-see BBC documentary called *Downfall* featuring interviews with key players). McDonnell Douglas executives infected the Boeing culture with a cost-obsessed 'make-do' attitude, leading to fundamental compromises on quality, design and safety, and ultimately the two horrific 737 Max crashes.

Even the great companies we talked about earlier haven't been immune throughout their history.

Ford in the 1970s. The company knowingly produced and sold the Pinto model with a defective fuel tank design which meant the tank could rupture and catch fire in a rear-end collision. Although internal company memos acknowledged the defect and its potential to cause fatalities, Ford executives decided against a recall, reasoning that it was more cost-effective to settle lawsuits than to fix the issue. It's a notorious example how Suits can get carried away, risking all the legal, reputational and human consequences.

Apple in the 1990s. The shareholders thought a more conventional business person could do better than Steve Jobs so they brought in a marketing guy from Pepsi. After he nearly ran Apple into the ground (using perfect-sounding business logic), they brought Jobs back to save the company.

WHEN TECHNICAL PEOPLE DON'T LISTEN TO 'THE SUITS', IT CAN LEAD TO FAILURE TO COMMERCIALIZE GREAT IDEAS, EXPENSIVE 'SCIENCE PROJECTS' WITH NO MARKET, AND EVEN THE FAILURE OF ONCE-GREAT BUSINESSES...

THE DEATH OF DEC: A GEEK-DRIVEN INSIDE JOB

Over thirty years, starting from 1957, founder and CEO Ken Olsen built the Digital Equipment Corporation to be the world's second largest computer manufacturer after IBM. When I was a university student in software engineering in the 1980s, DEC VAX minicomputers were the leading edge. DEC was an engineering and innovation-based culture where the engineers were the heroes and top executives.

Its answer to any marketing issue was to build another, even more sophisticated and costly piece of kit. And it worked – until the advent of the PC (a technologically boring product as they saw it).

When these desktop computers became a commodity, DEC knew that they had to develop a market-need driven strategy: building what customers needed rather than what got their engineers excited.

They knew it, but they just didn't want to do it. It would mean firing senior executives who weren't prepared to change. It would mean saying "no" to engineers with new ideas. It would mean emphasising customer research, service and software applications, rather than ever more glorious technology. So now, DEC is no more.

Xerox (at least in computing) didn't make a viable change either. They developed the mouse-and-windows user interface, but instead if commercialising it, they kept tinkering with new tech marvels. Apple and Microsoft built two of the world's most valuable companies using their ideas.

HOW IBM AVOIDED DIGITAL'S SAD FATE

Reinvention is hard, but not at all impossible

Interestingly, IBM managed to make the sort of leaps that eluded both Digital Equipment Corporation and Xerox. At the start of the 80s, IBM was prepared to build personal computers even as that accelerated the shift away from the mainframe market they had dominated.

And as the 1990s got underway, CEO Lou Gerstner recognised the threat posed by the commoditisation of computers. He saw that IBM's traditional focus on hardware was no longer sustainable. The future lay in providing comprehensive solutions integrating hardware, software, and services. Instead of resisting the shift in the market, IBM repurposed its unmatched expertise to better meet the evolving needs of enterprise customers.

TRIBAL WISDOM FROM SUITS ABOUT GEEKS

Geeks are more focused on tech for its own sake, and less on how it fits our strategy. "I've got key projects that are running behind and they're messing about with pet experiments."

Geeks love their technical jargon (and are they using it to bamboozle me?). "They're throwing around jargon and acronyms with no connection to the big picture of what we're trying to achieve. And I think they do it sometimes to create bullshit excuses just so I can't challenge them."

Geeks are too casual about deadlines. "We agree due dates and I'll think, 'Brilliant, we can work with that.' But then we get close to the deadline and they're nowhere near ready. I think about adding on a few weeks, just to be safe. But the risk is if they realise I'm doing that, it'll get even worse."

Geeks say, "But we've always done it this way". "They're supposed to be into new technology and stuff but it's really ironic: they hate change! They just don't want to budge. I get that they like their routine, but come on, we need to work in new ways. For such clever people it's idiotic."

Look... here's the problem with Geeks...

Geeks low ball the budget then give in to feature creep. "They're scared to say how much something will really cost so they give a low estimate. That means going over-budget is baked it from the start."

Geeks forget it's a business. "They make decisions that work technically, but they just don't fit with our business goals or what's happening in the market. We need to work on getting them to see the whole picture, not just the tech part."

Geeks over-engineer everything. "We need simpler solutions that we can actually handle and that won't drain our time and money."

Geeks have their heads in the sand about market changes. "Everything's moving at lightning speed in our industry. We've got to keep up. But I feel like our engineers just can't – or won't – switch gears quickly enough. Sometimes it's because they've fallen in love with an old technology and just can't let go. If we're too slow, we'll be dead in the water."

Geeks don't do their admin. "One engineer explained it to me like this: 'When a Geek has agreed to perform a task for a corporate admin function (such as short-list candidates, fill in an expense claim, do their performance appraisal) there is no need to remind them about it every six months!'"

Geeks seem to forget we actually have (human) customers. "They forget we're making stuff for real people. They're so into the tech side of things that they don't really think about how usable our products are or whether the features are really what's needed."

TRIBAL WISDOM FROM
GEEKS ABOUT SUITS

Oh yeah? Let me tell you about Suits.

Suits want the Earth. Yesterday. "It's really tough when they set these crazy deadlines and expect the impossible. They don't seem to get how complex engineering is and all the problems that can pop up out of nowhere..."

Suits want us to cheat the laws of physics, but they don't actually understand those laws. "They agree things with customers without understanding what it takes to get stuff to work. We deal with 'real' reality."

Suits just think short term. "It's all about quick wins and this quarter. We're being pushed to rush jobs and cut corners. You end up with a product that's not up to standard, and that's not what good engineering is about. Worst case you've got a 737 MAX."

Suits always want us to do "more with less". "We can't do a proper job when we don't have what we need. Trying to make something great with too little budget or the wrong tools just makes the job harder and the end result isn't what it could be."

Suits don't involve us in decisions. "We're kept out of the loop on big decisions. They commit us to things that are almost impossible. They don't understand – or want to understand – the constraints on the ground."

Suits talk in meaningless management-speak. "They talk in management-speak, and the only feedback we get is if we miss one of their unrealistic deadlines. A lot of the time around here, 'praise' is just the absence of criticism."

They don't want to pay for maintenance. "They don't grasp how much time and effort we need to keep our existing systems running smoothly. It piles up risks down the line."

Suits are always into some new fad they found in a book at the airport or heard about from a random stranger at a conference."We start a lot of management initiatives but don't finish them. It starts with an enthusiastic kick-off and then things get quietly abandoned."

Suits stick their noses into stuff they don't understand. "To be fair, my boss was an engineer a long time ago, but he hasn't kept up to date so he has crap ideas."

Suits don't care about our career development. "To be honest my direct boss doesn't want me to go on courses because they want to keep me in my current role."

"

We're talking about people who see the world differently.

THE VALUE OF ACHIEVING COMMERCIAL–TECHNICAL SYNERGY

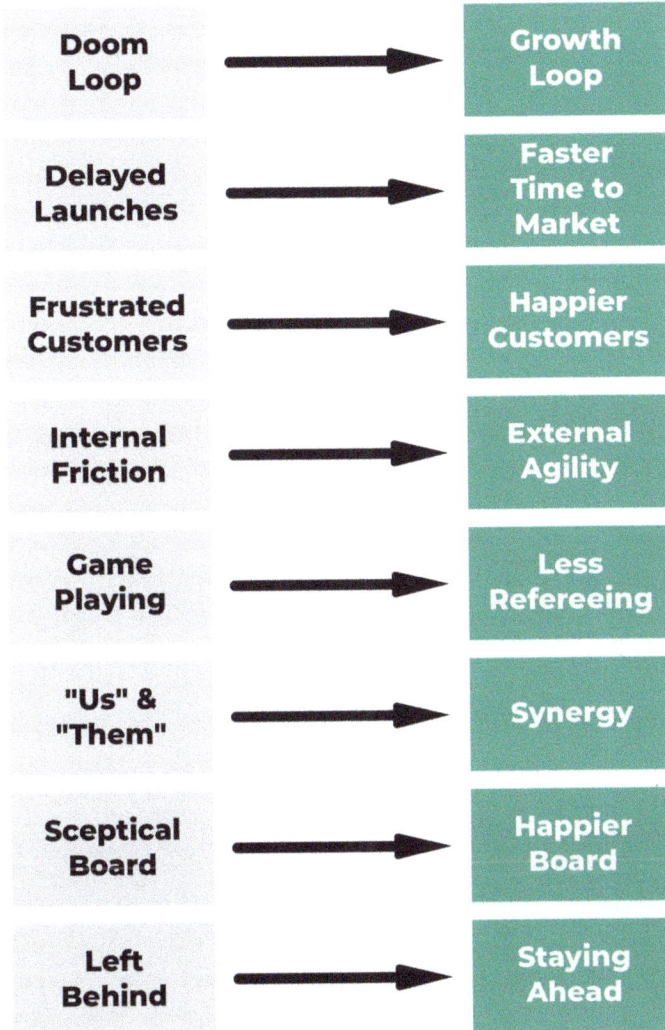

Doom Loop	→ Growth Loop
Delayed Launches	→ Faster Time to Market
Frustrated Customers	→ Happier Customers
Internal Friction	→ External Agility
Game Playing	→ Less Refereeing
"Us" & "Them"	→ Synergy
Sceptical Board	→ Happier Board
Left Behind	→ Staying Ahead

"Working with you, not against each other"

PROBLEMS YOU CAN AVOID

It's not just the bickering you can stop: Suits vs Geeks Doom Loops can have big effects on the business. These are avoidable costs. The three biggest problems are:

1) Unfocused strategy that's easy for competitors to outmanoeuvre

- Suits might try to achieve cost leadership by cutting quality, rather than by building a unique activity system. They might try to create differentiation through exaggeration (Empty Suits making empty promises). Either way, trust is damaged and revenue is lost.

- Geeks might suppose they know more about what the customers should have than the customers does themselves. Or they might spend months building a product no customer cares about.

2) Slow or inadequate execution that damages your reputation

- Suits might be pushy so that corners get cut (as per Boeing). They might exaggerate their sales projections and hope in vain they can make up their quota in the closing days of the quarter.

- Geeks might deliberately over-estimate the time required to deliver something so as to build in a cushion, or spend endless time debating marginally different courses of action, or shoring up huge defences against marginal risks.

3) An unmanageable organization

The games that Suits and Geeks play create a Hall of Mirrors that makes delivering results a tricky business. It can be hard to deliver on commitments, and you might even secretly wonder if you'll end up taking the blame.

> We can't dictate our customers' tech choices the way we used to. We have to be market driven

> But sometimes the customer wants the impossible, and you promise it them just to get the sale

The way these two are talking, it looks like an impossible dilemma. And when both sides dig in, it *is* impossible!

Unfortunately, a lot of well-intentioned attempts to break the dilemma just make it worse. We'll see how it happens in the next section. That way, you'll know the trip-wires and traps to avoid.

"We've survived while our competitors gave in to pressure to cut prices because our people have worked together across the organization to understand what our customers really value. Engineering excellence, yes. But also, we understand their hassles, we design for the situations they really find themselves in, we get stuff to people when we say we will. They'll pay for things like that."

Aerospace executive

Part Two

Fixes That Fail

MAYBE YOU'VE ALREADY TRIED...

The two most popular ways to try to end the blame games and all their attendant problems in the hope or reestablishing growth are:

- **Tightening governance**. It seems logical but it never seems to get the results to justify the extra effort.

- **"Improving communication"** – It can seem helpful during the workshops, but not much sticks. Everyone is nicer until the next crunch comes.

Remember we're talking about people who see the world rather differently:

How a Suit sees a 2x2 Matrix.   **How a Geek sees a 2x2 Matrix*.**

* If you don't get this, you are very unlikely to be a Geek.

We kid ourselves into thinking we can make one tribe act like the other.

DON'T TRY AND CONVERT GEEKS INTO SUITS (OR VICE VERSA)

Remember:

> ## Comprehension is not a requisite of cooperation.

OK if you're a real Geek, you'll recognise where that quote comes from. *Matrix Reloaded*, right? But what does it mean?

Well, let's continue the Geek-fest and get a great example from *Return of the Jedi*, the third film of the original *Star Wars* trilogy. In a pivotal section, the heroes led by Luke Skywalker are captured by a tribe of hostile bear-like warriors called the Ewoks. There seems every possibility that the Ewoks intend to feast on their prisoners. Fortunately for Luke and his band, however, his loyal protocol droid C3P0 is mistaken by the Ewoks for some sort of messiah whose arrival is predicted by their tribal mythology. He is accorded the awe and respect appropriate for a divine being and proceeds to use his position to enrol the support of the Ewoks in Luke's bid to rescue Princess Leia from the evil forces of the Empire. They fight alongside our heroes, and their commitment is decisive in securing victory.

Imagine if Luke asked C3PO to explain all about the Empire and the Rebellion and to try to persuade the Ewoks to fight. The Ewoks could easily have responded with "not our fight" and carried on to eat our heroes.

If you present an initiative so that it fits your audience's world they are more likely to support it, even if they don't understand your way of thinking about it. What matters is that you understand **their** way of thinking about it.

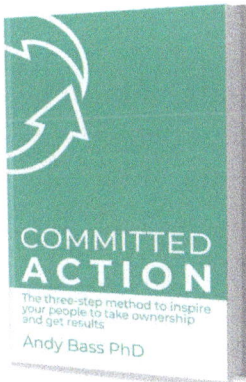

For more about this, have a look at my book, *Committed Action: the three-step method to inspire your people to take ownership and get results.*

NAÏVE CONSULTING APPROACHES TO THE PROBLEM JUST MAKE IT WORSE

Frustratingly, the suggestions you get from consultants often make things worse. Among those consultants, there are two broad schools: those that believe in what I call *Management by Algorithm* and those with *Organizational Development Delusion*.

Management by Algorithm assumes that the human side of business can all be reduced to processes and procedures

Those with Organization Development Delusion think that if we buy into the same woo-woo values, everything will work out fine

MANAGEMENT BY ALGORITHM ('MBA')

Consultants who believe in 'MBA' love their boxes and arrows. They think that you can change an organization by changing its structure. They'll tell you, 'What gets measured gets done'. They might recommend productivity software to reduce everyone's wiggle room.

'MBA' appeals to engineering-oriented firms because it treats management like engineering. Now, some aspects of management can be treated like engineering; but not leadership and culture.

Treating humans as a cog in machine might work in a logistics warehouse where people are basically putting up with it, but it won't work with engineers who need to think and act for themselves to be effective.

Management by Algorithm triggers direct resistance. It's like Newton's Second Law of Motion: you push and they push back. If you try to boss clever people around you'll create active resistance and secret 'Pet Projects' and Shadow IT. You end up feeling like you're pushing a rock up a hill.

Claudio Ciborra said this about box-and-arrow methods:
"Contrary to their promise, they are deceivingly abstract and removed from practice. Everyone can experience this when he or she moves from the models to the implementation phase."

One executive had a lightbulb moment after I'd fed back the results of interviews with his teams. He told me, "We're trying to apply the kind of governance we use for manufacturing operations to our strategy process. It can't work, because it isn't making room for the insights, the fast failures, the conversational dead-ends, the uncertainty".

ORGANIZATIONAL DEVELOPMENT DELUSION (O.D.D.)

Other consultants suffer from what I call, "Organizational Development Delusion" or 'O.D.D'. They believe that if everyone would just agree to play nice, everything will be fine. They act as if going to work is a Hero's Journey. They love personality tests, team-building, pop psychology and shared values. They grab bits of half-understood psychology and neuroscience and run workshops that seem to have little effect on the ground. In the worst case, you will find charlatans, but even among the sincere, there are many who stretch psychological research far beyond its limits. They've never heard of the 'replication crisis' in academic psychology (many peer-reviewed research findings have turned out to be false, often because people got the statistics wrong, and sometimes, because they just made them up!).

Some O.D.D. initiatives don't even get out of the gate, especially if they can be labelled 'Woo Woo." Both Suits AND Geeks will roll their eyes if there's any suggestion of that. But there are some more insidious problems:

1. **The 'Be Spontaneous' paradox:** when you try to get people to 'buy in' to organizational values, it often feels a bit weird. You're inviting lip-service because people can't really say 'No'. You're saying, "I don't want you to do things the way I say because I want you to do it. I want you to do it because YOU want to do it." It's like asking someone to be spontaneous on a count of three!

2. **The Empowerment Paradox:** if I can empower you, then I can presumably reverse my decision at some point and disempower you. Empowerment is a hard trick for most leaders to pull off with credibility.

3. **The credibility gap between what you say and do:** In the jargon, this is the difference between the organization's "Espoused beliefs" – what it says it believes, which is always very wholesome – and its "Theory-in-use" – the beliefs it acts on in reality.

   If you ask people to buy in to shared values, you will absolutely never get away with violating those values, or tolerating anyone else doing so (no matter how good their numbers).

   Geeks in particular are very sensitive to mismatches between words and deeds. Any such mismatch undermines leadership credibility and corrodes the culture.

> *When you go down the O.D.D. route, you feel like you're having to be 'nice', and they feel patronised.*

The more you try to force the change, the more things stay the same.

The more they pull, the more they're trapped:
One or both have got to get (carefully) back in the boat.
Adapted from Watzlawick, Weakland & Fisch, CHANGE: Principles of Problem Formation and Problem Resolution.

It's a bit like the two sailors in the picture. They're in the same boat, trying their best as it seems from their point of view, but in a way that makes things more unstable.

All the attention, energy and effort is directed at internal foolishness rather than at navigating the external world.

'TRIBAL WISDOM' FUELS THE TRAP

One manufacturer was on the verge of bankruptcy due to quality problems. In interviews, commercial managers and engineers expressed the kind of 'Tribal Wisdom about Suits & Geeks' that we met earlier. The diagram show how their beliefs about each other interlocked. In each case, what one side framed as good, the other framed as bad. This created a kind of deadly embrace of Us and Them.

	According to ENGINEERS. . .	According to MANAGERS. . .
ENGINEERS. . .	Are precise, deal in technical calculations, use technical criteria, have technical competence, judge success in terms of solving technical problems	Are nitpicking, can't grasp strategic issues, are upstarts, present conflicting data, are out of touch with the commercial world
MANAGERS. . .	Fudge, are bureaucratic, lie, prioritise money over being correct, are expedient	See the big picture, think strategically, prioritise the health of the business, interpret data, make judgment calls

The more the Geeks criticised the Suits for prioritising money over precision, the more the Suits were convinced the Geeks were out of touch with commercial reality. The more the Suits accused the Geeks of nitpicking, the more the Geeks were contemptuous of the Suits' lack of technical understanding.

As long as each side saw the other in these limited ways, they were caught in a trap with no clear options for escape. In fact whatever solutions they came up with were likely to reinforce perceptions rather than ease them. For example, if managers fired the 'guilty' engineers and tightened up procedures, that would just be seen as more bureaucracy, expedience and fudging. That's just a recipe for resistance.

THE TRAP HOLDS A DOOM LOOP IN PLACE

Doom loops are easy to trigger

The potential for a Doom loop is inherent in the differences between Suits and Geeks. The interventions that we discussed – whether 'MBA' or O.D.D. – tighten the trap. You can't eliminate the potential for Doom Loops, you can only steer round it.

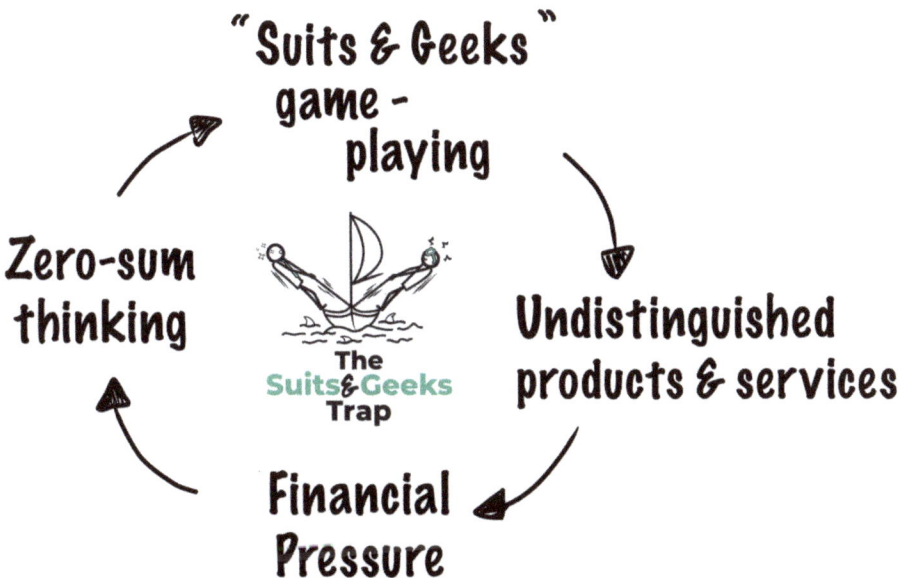

"Suits & Geeks" game - playing

Undistinguished products & services

Financial Pressure

Zero-sum thinking

The Suits & Geeks Trap

ESCAPING
THE TRAP

Fortunately, there is hope. There must be, right? You've seen great tech-based companies grow and thrive. You've probably experienced it yourself. It's easy to forget once the Blame Games gets going that Suits and Geeks bring strengths the other group needs in order to thrive: that's the foundation for Growth Loops and the great successes we discussed at the start of the book.

Each Tribe's 'wisdom' is biased towards the negative tendencies of the other tribe. A fairer appraisal would recognise that everyone has both positive and negative tendencies, and Suits and Geeks are no different.

THE LIGHT AND DARK SIDES OF SUITS & GEEKS

Remember we're stereotyping, but it's a good place to start:

	GEEKS	SUITS
At their BEST (Nurtures Growth Loops)	Ingenious Innovative (with technology) Create Value Rigorous Eclectic	Customer-oriented Innovative (with business models) Capture Value Action-oriented Flexible
At their WORST (Drives Doom Loops)	Procrastinating Perfectionist Rigid Unaware/uninterested in customers Indecisive	Rent-seeking Political Game-playing Expedient Greedy

The skilled leader has to foster the positive qualities and discourage the negative qualities. Fortunately, the positive qualities can be self-reinforcing.

Accentuate the Positive!

THEY'RE NOT *JUST* SUITS (OR GEEKS)

I started out by acknowledging that there is truth in the stereotypes. But...

Have you ever been stunned to learn a fact about a co-worker that shattered an assumption you had about them? Here are some of the ones I've come across:

- A gentle policy researcher whose hobby was white-collar boxing.
- A school administrator who had long jumped for Great Britain.
- A clinical psychologist who had toured internationally as a backing singer for acts such as Paul Weller and Foreigner.
- An engineer who lived on a smallholding where he bred sheep.
- An introverted computer scientist who played lead guitar in a rock band that regularly played to hordes of tattooed Harley-Davidson-riding bikers.
- A banker who, despite no formal training in the subject, was a regular and active participant in weekly astrophysics seminars at one of the world's top universities.
- A temporary secretary who solved the final clue in a cryptic crossword that had baffled two computer science professors.

No doubt you can make your own list, and it's a great exercise to do so. It can remind you of how restricted our views of others and their talents can be.

Part Three

Do What Works

INSTEAD OF SUITS AND GEEKS, THINK 'MANAGERS & MAKERS'

Paul Graham's classic blog post "Maker's Schedule, Manager's Schedule" delves into the distinct ways that makers (creative professionals like programmers, engineers, writers, and designers) and managers (at all levels) structure their work time. Understanding this can transform your perspective on how work gets done in your organization.

Maker's Schedule

Makers require long, uninterrupted blocks of time to achieve the kind of focus which is essential for creative work. Their productivity hinges on these extended periods without interruptions. If a manager schedules a single meeting or interrupts with a 'quick question' it can derail their progress for an entire day. It's really tough to regain a previous level of concentration and sometimes great ideas are lost – very frustrating!

Manager's Schedule

In contrast, managers operate on a schedule segmented into short blocks of time. Their day is often filled with meetings, emails, and various forms of communication. This fragmentation is inherent to their role, and interruptions do less harm because their tasks are naturally broken into shorter, manageable chunks. Managers are accustomed to switching contexts throughout the day.

While Geeks are more often on the Maker's schedule and Suits are more often on the Manager's schedule, it isn't always so. You can be more flexible and develop more understanding if you realise it.

MANAGERS
MAKERS

Conflict Between Schedules

Both schedules makes sense but they can lead to conflict. Managers might schedule meetings without considering the significant impact on a maker's productivity. Makers then feel their valuable creative time is being chopped to bits, while managers feel their need for check-ins and updates is being disrespected.

Some tactics:

- **Talk about it!** Once everyone understands their different needs, they can usually come up with some simple improvements.
- **Designate times for meetings that accommodate both schedules**. For instance, holding meetings at the beginning or, better, the end of the day can help minimise disruptions to a maker's flow.
- **Maximise blocks of protected 'Maker time'.** Ideally have Maker Time Days (where makers are protected to get on with their work) and Manager Time Days (densely packed with the meetings and calls required for coordination).
- **If days must be mixed, schedule meetings by working back from the end of the day.** Alex Hormozi suggests you fill meeting slots in reverse order (so if you want to be finished by six, schedule a meeting for 17:30, then if another request comes it, schedule that one for 17:00 etc.

Understanding and respecting the differences between maker's and manager's schedules can massively reduce frustration and increase productivity.

THE LEADER MUST
RISE ABOVE

However hard you try, you may *never* get your Suits & Geeks to agree to see the world the same way. The good news is you don't need them to (remember Luke Skywalker and the Ewoks). But you do still need them to work together in the same direction.

To get this to happen, the first step is be able to see where all these people are coming from. Here's an intuitive and effective way to do it. The diagram represents some of the typical tensions in a tech-based organization in the form of a "Rich Picture" (a term coined by its originator, Peter Checkland). It's a great way to rise above the personalities and see the different points of view and motivations of the people who get caught in the games.

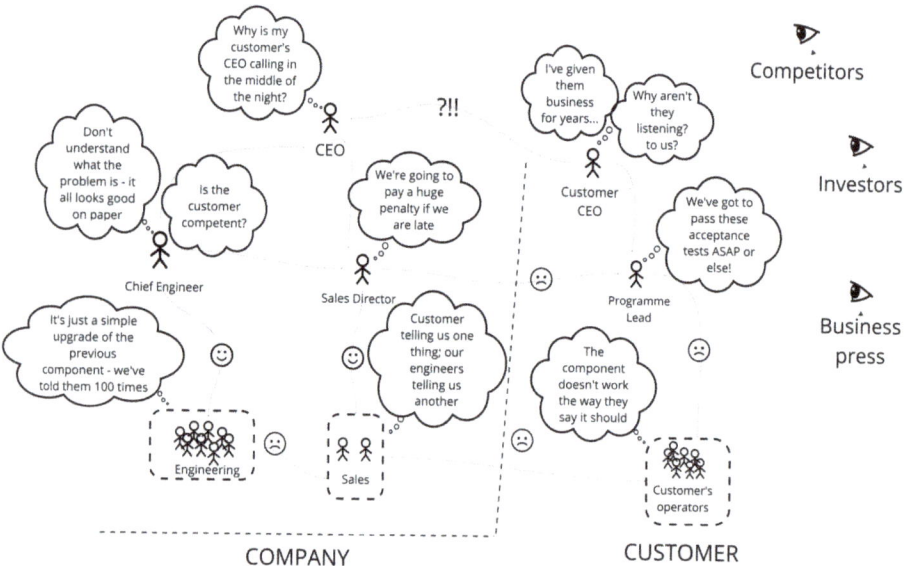

A Rich Picture give the parties a new perspective

The idea is simple, but the effect is powerful. Individuals and groups are represented as "stick people", their concerns, interests and objectives are captured in thought-bubbles, alliances and conflicts are labelled with smiles or frowns swords, and influential observers (media, regulatory authorities etc.) are shown by eyeballs. Beyond these basics, you can make up further elements as you go.

Once you've externalised the situation:

- it becomes less a matter of 'Us and Them".
- the picture starts to represent 'our shared problem'.
- you can check whether or not people are operating on the basis of reality or careless assumptions.

GET AT LEAST THREE PERSPECTIVES

There are more than two sides!

Building up a Rich Picture, and, in particular, finding out what goes into those thought-bubbles, is incredibly useful when you're thinking about leverage points in your organization.

If you take nothing else from this book, make a Rich Picture of the situation and reflect on its implications. This can be done very informally on a decent sized piece of paper, like a flipchart pad, and it's sure to provide you with valuable insights for improvement.

One thing you will likely learn is that you don't know enough about the interests of the people in your organization.

You want to get *at least* three perspectives:

1. Suit View
2. Geek View
3. Helicopter view

Some questions to consider:

1. Which managers could usefully spend time with which engineers?
2. Who else needs to meet whom?
3. Who are the pivotal people?
4. Who are the informal opinion leaders?
5. What's the potential for shadowing and exchanges?

A LEADER WHO ROSE ABOVE

A B2B IT company I know turned something that "everybody knows" is a problem into a quick boost to revenue, profits and loyalty. It's an approach that could work for a lot of other companies too.

Here's what happened. Those naughty salespeople, who "everybody knows" will do anything to make sales regardless of profit, had been sweetening deals by offering high-value customers unofficial access to tech support – direct phone numbers of technical gurus allowing customers to bypass the call centre, direct feeds of ticket-tracking information, that sort of thing.

On discovering these practices, the CFO was, shall we say, less than impressed ("Over-serving the customer! Cost!").

But the CFO manifested a Buddha-like serenity compared to the CIO, who was positively apoplectic ("Shadow systems!! RISK!!"). The President however saw it completely differently ("Hidden, but easy-to-address customer needs: opportunity!").

The company brought these unofficial practices out of the shadows, packaged them up as options to their traditional services, formalised the processes to provide proper governance, and offered them for sale.

The additional value to the customer, and so the price, was far higher than the corresponding additional cost, providing a nice quick bump to profitable revenues, and no resistance to implementation, since the company was doing it already.

TAP INTO EXISTING MOTIVATIONS

I have news: **You can't motivate people!** In truth, people are *already* motivated – even the ones you think are not.

The laziest good-for-nothing is motivated: to avoid hassle, responsibility and effort. You can *move* them with threats or bribes, but that's as good as it will get until they decide their priorities have changed.

On the other hand, your best employee is also motivated: perhaps to pursue a rewarding career, contribute to an exciting, worthwhile enterprise or support family members.

These motivations are there already; a good leader taps into them.

The intrinsic nature of motivation means that if you want real commitment you can't get it using extrinsic factors such as pay and perks alone. You need to make the work meaningful for people *the way that makes sense to them.*

You need to connect the dots: from what you want them to do, to their existing motivations.

Remember...

"Suits needs technology to make money.

Geeks need money to make technology."

MOTIVATION IS INTRINSIC

Because people have a wide range of perspectives and interests, they will respond to the same situation in a wide variety of ways. However hard you try (and, boy, do people try) you may never get them to agree to see the world the same way. The good news is you don't need them to (remember Luke Skywalker and the Ewoks). But you do still need them to work together in the same direction.

For example, present commercial factors as engineering challenges: when I was working with a bunch of automotive engineers on how they could help improve profitability, I didn't talk about "DuPont Ratios" for calculating return on capital.

Instead of using the language of finance, I talked about,"Tuning the Profit Engine." I likened businesses with with high inventory turns to fast-revving but low-torque motorcycle engines, and high margin businesses with low cash velocity to high-torque, low-revving truck engines.

They quickly became fascinated – and a lot more help to the business – not because they were interested in business profitability (some were, some weren't), but because they loved reasoning about engines!

ENLIST THE HELP OF YOUR CUSTOMERS!

Invite your customers' decision-makers to talk to your staff.

Five reasons to do it:

1. **Customers are more believable.** When they talk about how much they need quality, on-time delivery and service, it carries a lot more weight than if you say it. Customers are not seen as having any ulterior motive such as boosting their bonuses.
2. **Employees love to hear that their work is appreciated by customers.** Mostly they don't get any feedback. Even if they do, taking the boss's word for it is never as compelling as hearing it direct from the customer
3. **Customers really enjoy it.** It's a massive compliment that you value their opinion so much. They'll feel like a celebrity. It's the cheat-code for strengthening your relationship.
4. **It's very easy and inexpensive.** If they can't attend in person, see if you can get them to speak on video.
5. **You can chat to your customers while making the arrangements and showing them around.** You'll pick up insights and opportunities that your competitors will miss out on.

Bring your customers inside seems so obvious. But when I suggest it, people often look at me like I've got two heads (if they tell the truth, it's because it sounds scary). When you do it though, the effect is amazing. It'll fire people up like you won't believe.

LET YOUR PEOPLE HEAR THE CUSTOMER TALK

McCain Foods faced a tough innovation challenge: how do you come up with anything new in the area of 'frozen products made of potato that you can buy in a supermarket'?

On the face of it, this was not an area ripe for new ideas. Internal people thought they knew all the angles in this business, and weren't particularly open to hearing anything new. It wasn't arrogance, they just didn't think there was anything new to hear. Aided by, among others, my colleague Jack Martin Leith, McCain held Open Space meetings with consumers.

The wrinkle was that they invited key internal people to attend as 'witnesses'. To their surprise, the witnesses gained all kinds of insights about how their products were viewed, and they came up with a range of new ideas, two of which became high-selling profitable new products for McCain.

Some of the most resistant internal people were highly enthused by the approach and became vociferous champions for these new initiatives.

GET YOUR PEOPLE (ESPECIALLY THE GEEKS) OUT OF THE BUILDING*

The sales team of a marine propulsion company was getting badly beaten up by their customer, a ship-builder. The situation was so bad that the company's engineers were refusing to respond to the customer's calls.

Finally the customer's CEO, Tom, called the company's CEO, Dan. Tom was incandescent with rage. He needed to deliver a ship to a very demanding end customer, but his team couldn't get the propulsion system to pass a particular test involving access to an inspection panel. Huge payments were being held up. Tom wanted the chief engineer's head.

Dan went to his engineers with Tom's complaint. They said, "Not bloody Tom again! He wants everyone to bow down to him because he's their CEO. He has no understanding. It just takes a simple Allen key to open the inspection panel! We've told our salesman a million times."

The engineering team saw Tom as a loudmouthed Suit! A business man; not on their intellectual level. But they had never actually met Tom. They had no idea he was a naval architect who had been designing and building ships for four decades!

Their view was that the new motor was just a higher-performance evolution of a design they had supplied to Tom several times before, and it was brilliant. Any problems were clearly the fault of Tom's team.

So Dan took his chief engineer, Simon, on a long-haul flight to visit the customer. To his amazement he discovered that Simon had NEVER visited a customer on site in his twelve years at the company.

*Steve Blank's famous exhortation to entrepreneurs cutting themselves off from customers.

In front of his team, Tom tried to follow Simon's instructions for opening the panel, but quickly gave up. "If it's so easy, you do it" he said. Simon stepped forward. And he couldn't do it! A bulkhead was in the way. The bulkhead was in the specification drawings, but for some reason had been ignored as a factor (because it wasn't part of the engine, and this engineer only thought about engines, not the cramped conditions in the ship)!

Once he had seen the issue, Simon and his team quickly redesigned a portion of casing to reposition the access panel, and everything was resolved.

> "
> Value resides in the mind of the customer. You won't understand it if you spend all your time in the office. You need a different perspective. Andy's book will encourage you to get out and find one.
>
> Rory Sutherland, Advertising Industry Legend and Vice-Chairman, Ogilvy, in the Foreword to my book, *Start With What Works: a faster way to grow your business*"

WATCH OUT FOR PERVERSE INCENTIVES

How a boss nearly undermined a new initiative

I was working with a pharmaceutical distribution business that needed to innovate fast. Drugs were coming off-patent, and industry forces were going to change who made money and how. The MD was worried. He was also frustrated that his senior managers, who he described as excellent operations people, were failing to come up with innovative responses to the new needs of their customers. As we discussed his objectives, he painted a clear picture of how he wanted these managers to innovate.

Then he said, "But they damn well better still hit their monthly KPIs."

This was just not going to work.

Why? Well put yourself in the shoes of the managers. The incentives are clearly to keep operating well and not to worry about the innovation.

Here's what goes on in their heads: "If I try to innovate, I'll have to find the extra time by working longer hours, and I may well fail. Whatever people say, that will probably be held against me later. But if I just keep on operating, all that will happen is I will get whinged at by the MD. Big deal. It's not a sacking offence is it? Anyway, I know the system really well. They need me to make sure the drugs get delivered. On the other hand, if I MISS my KPIs, then I'll have real trouble."

Only by changing the incentives could the MD hope to get these managers to give innovation some serious attention.

	If I DO?	If I DON'T?
What WILL happen…	Better? or Riskier?	Better? or Riskier?
What WON'T happen…	Better? or Riskier?	Better? or Riskier?

As long as I sell something I get my bonus. If you can't deliver, it won't affect me.

It's fun and low-stress to research new techniques. My boss gets frustrated that progress is slow but he needs me.

IMPROVE THROUGH WORK, NOT WORKSHOPS

Training workshops are of limited value in getting people to collaborate and engage with an agenda. They're especially inadequate when it comes to changing attitudes.

People rely on training events because they seem easy to manage – you book a room, hire a trainer with some generic knowledge that supposedly relates to your problem, get people to show up, give them tea and coffee, and then get them to fill in 'feedback forms' which supposedly 'evaluate' the training.

Actually the feedback from workshops is often a bit of a game played by training managers and training providers. A moment's objective thought should show that just because the trainees find the workshop useful or interesting, that's NO guarantee it will impact on behaviour and performance.

On some level therefore, many managers have become extremely cynical about the value from training programmes, especially of the 'soft skills' variety. They are tired of 'ra-ra' sessions, guru-inspired fads, outward bound courses and other ideas which don't relate in any obvious way to the workplace. Even the best traditional classroom-based training is a problem, because the simple truth is that people in the real world don't behave the same way as people in training rooms.

> Training workshops can be useful tools, but just as nutritional supplements need to be "part of a balanced diet", workshops can only help in the context of doing new things 'for real.'

How do you foster engagement and collaboration if training won't do it? In essence, by putting people together on substantive tasks which require enhanced collaboration skills, and providing the right kind of support as they develop ways of working together.

With a real task, collaboration issues will inevitably surface and be seen as relevant, providing 'emerging targets' for focused learning. The beauty of the approach is that the learning context is real. There's no need to figure out how to transfer it from a classroom. And people are being productive, rather than being taken out of their jobs.

"But if we use a real task, what happens when people make mistakes?"

People inevitably will make mistakes. But you know what? People returning from training courses make mistakes too, often without access to the trainer to check and discuss their actions (and very often their manager has little idea what new things they learned on the course that they are now tempted to try).

On the other hand, mistake made within the kind of supportive framework I'm talking about can be managed and transformed into powerful, relevant learning opportunities.

TRANSFORMING A FACTORY IN MEXICO WITHOUT TRAINING WORKSHOPS (AND WITHOUT SPEAKING SPANISH)

Here was the problem. My client – the English President of a US manufacturer – had a plant in Mexico. It was an untidy, oily mess. Quality, on-time delivery and safety were all concerns.

We transformed the plant with a two hour meeting.

How? By getting everyone (I mean everyone) from the shop-floor together in a warehouse, setting things up right, and then asking the assembled crowd the following incredibly sophisticated and magical question (through an interpreter!):

"How do we improve the plant?"

Result? Stark improvements in quality, delivery, reduced accidents – not to mention more pleasant working conditions and clean, tidy facilities you'd be proud to show your customers around.

Sounds good, but the problem I hear is, "When we ask the people closest to the action they don't come up with any decent ideas. They say nothing or just complain about the cafeteria."

The trick is in the set up. I'll usually coach the plant manager to say something like this to their people:

"Look. Forget how we've handled this kind of thing in the past. I know we might have asked for suggestions but then ignored them. I really want your ideas. Here's how I'll handle them:

- If an idea makes sense and we can afford to, we'll just do it.
- If it's a good idea and we don't have the money, I will take it to the CEO and advocate for it. I can't guarantee we'll get everything, but I will explain if we don't.
- And look, if I think it's a bad idea, I'll just say why I think so and we can talk about it."

Disarming, direct setups like this make a difference that many managers find unbelievable. The shop-floor love being taken seriously. They don't even mind if you can't implement all their ideas if you explain why. Your people already have the answers to many of your problems. But you have to ask them in language they'll respond to.

Part Four

Strategy, Execution, Leadership

SUITS, GEEKS AND STRATEGY

Big strategic dangers for Suits

- Misunderstanding how value is created by 'cost leadership' business models, leading to zealous cost cutting to hit short term profit targets (Boeing's fatal problem).
- Sacrificing design in order to reduce time-to-market.
- Buying your way into a market with low bids then hoping to increase prices later.

Big strategic dangers for Geeks

- Over-engineering and so adding excessive cost.
- Making things too complicated (think "Alexa-enabled washing machine", or "WiFi connected microwave").
- Spending lots of time on refinements and features the customer doesn't notice (hence are not *actually* differentiating).

MAN Trucks, working with Hoyer, the fuel distributiom business, discovered that Hoyer wasn't interested in the diminishing marginal gains in fuel efficiency that its engineers were proudly working on. Why? Because the incremental saving was a tiny part of customers' operating budget. Much bigger influences on the customer's profitability include driver absence due to backache, and truck availability at the right location.

Understanding Hoyer's real issues suggested various innovations including not only traditional product options such as ergonomic seating, but also the idea of "truck availability as a service".

Getting Suits and Geeks to work together to produce value-amplifying differentiation.

The strategic dangers on the preceding page are refections of "The Dark Side of Suits and Geeks" we met earlier (Page 52). The solution lies in tapping into the Light Side shown on the same diagram. That way, you benefit from both the customer-focused insights of your commercial people *and* the ingenuity of your technology people.

For more examples, see my book *Start With What Works: a faster way to grow your business.*.

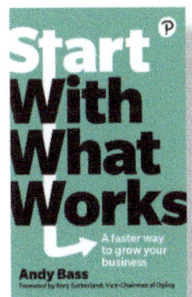

SUITS, GEEKS AND DELIVERY

How they slow things down

SUITS	GEEKS
Allowing customers to keep changing specifications Over promising, so that the Geeks have got an impossible task Creating mistrust by sandbagging	Unnecessary gold plating Dysfunctional perfectionism Procrastination

How they can help speed things up

SUITS	GEEKS
Smooth out and mediate difficult relationships between customer and company staff	Apply their ingenuity to improve processes Automation, design for manufacture

"

Suits rush in while
Geeks prepare to start
to get ready to begin to
change.

BARRIERS TO EXECUTION

What stops strategy being successfully executed? The most common barriers include:

1) **Three kinds of "Preparing to get ready to start to do it soon but not yet"**:
   a.) **Unnecessary interim goals:** "Let's do Y in preparation for doing Z". "OK, in which case, we really need to do X" first.
   b.) **Unnecessary prerequisite problem-solving:** "We can't get started on Z until we've solved problem P"
   c.) **Blaming an external cause (Us and Them):** "We're completely up for doing Z, but THEY are preventing us."

2) **Unclear communication of plans** e.g. assuming people were clear on What, Why, Who, When.

3) **Poor tracking and follow-up.** It's easy to put following up off until tomorrow, especially if chasing someone feels like it will lead to an uncomfortable conversation.

4) **Inadequate 'plan protection'** – hoping the plans will work out as they do on paper/on-screen, rather than anticipating problems and developing preventative and contingent actions to ensure progress isn't blocked when things go sideways in the real world.

5) **Not protecting priorities** e.g. it's always easy to find good reasons to delay the "important but not urgent" and simply human nature to avoid tasks which might be anticipated to be unpleasant or uncomfortable.

Priorities for the Leader

Know and address the foibles of both Suits & Geeks.

- Watch out for the three kinds of preparing to get ready to start to change – this is particularly a Geek issue.

- Communication of plans. Connect the dots for people (see my book, *Committed Action: The three-step method to inspire your people to take ownership and get results*). In my experience, leaders often think that plans and their rationales are more obvious than they turn out to be to those who need to carry them out.

- Tracking and follow-up. There's a balance to strike here. Too much governance can slow down a project just as surely as not enough.

- Plan protection. Geeks will want to overdo this, and Suits will want to take more risk. Again, it's the leader's job to find the balance.

- Prioritisation. People prioritise according to their incentives. Make sure the incentives support your plans.

COMMITTED
A C T I O N
The three-step method to inspire
your people to take ownership
and get results
Andy Bass PhD

SUITS, GEEKS AND LEADERSHIP

Broad context

Deep expertise

We all start out developing deep expertise in one area of business – it could be sales, engineering, finance etc. Then as we develop, we need to understand the broader context, and become increasingly conversant with other areas. Some people get this. Others don't.

A well-developed leader could have come from any specialism, and will ideally be more than conversant with all main areas of business.

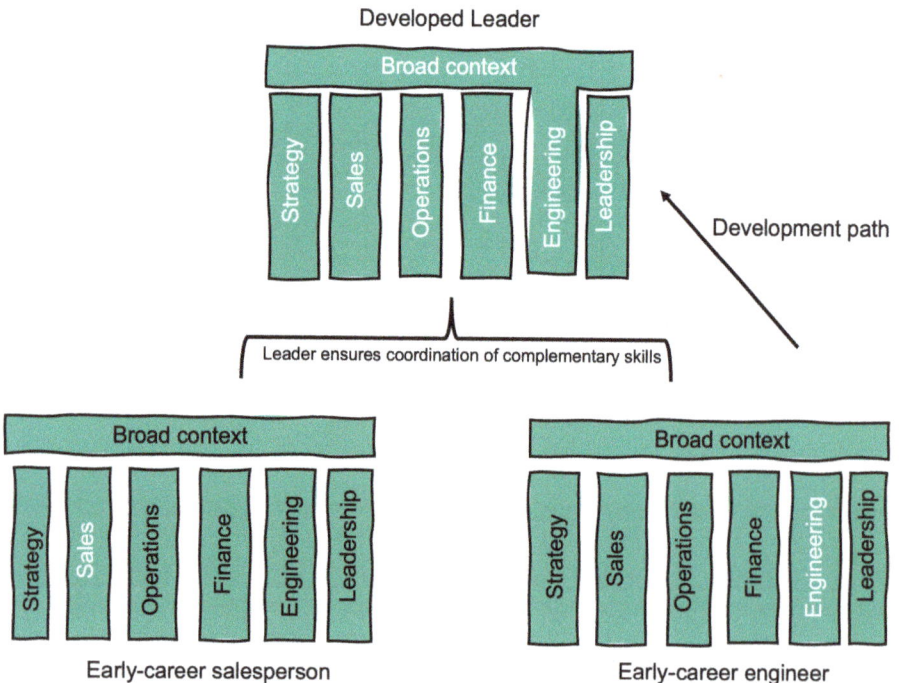

Developed Leader

Broad context

Strategy | Sales | Operations | Finance | Engineering | Leadership

Development path

Leader ensures coordination of complementary skills

Broad context

Strategy | Sales | Operations | Finance | Engineering | Leadership

Early-career salesperson

Broad context

Strategy | Sales | Operations | Finance | Engineering | Leadership

Early-career engineer

THE LEADER'S JOB

The well-developed leader understands how all the pieces fit together. They are no longer tribal.

They have to:

- Integrate people of varying levels and breadths of knowledge.
- Educate people on the need to develop not only depth but also breadth.
- Acknowledge that people are at different stages and have different comfort zones.

You can't expect to get every Geek to embrace commercial awareness, marketing or leadership any more than you can get all Suits to become engineers or financial wizards.

And neither do you want them all to. You want a mixture of generalists and specialists. You also want some extreme specialists.

If they are...

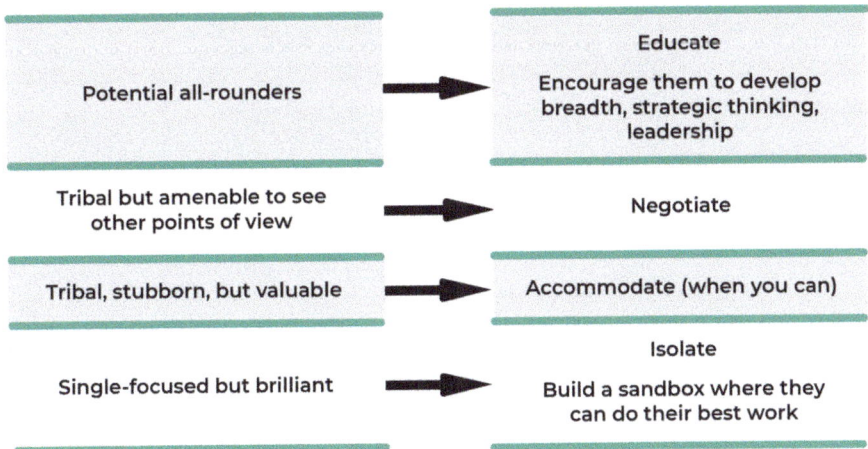

Part Five

What To Do Next

TEN WAYS TO ESCAPE THE SUITS & GEEKS TRAP

1. **Appeal to the wildly different mindsets of engineers and managers.** Remember: 'Suits' need technology to make money. 'Geeks' need money to make technology.

2. **Don't try and change people's motivations.** You can't motivate people – they're already motivated. Appeal to what they're already interested in, and already turned off by.

3. **Stop pursuing 'solutions' that actually make things worse.** The tools consultants use can exacerbate the problem because they make people feel pushed or patronised. And people are very creative in how they resist being pushed.

4. **Sort out your top team relationships.** Any Suit v Geek issues on the leadership team will be reflected in 'proxy battles' around the rest of the organization.

5. **Don't make people sing 'Kumbaya'.** It's a guaranteed recipe for cynicism.

6. **Start with what works.** Turn exceptions into interventions. Where do your Suits and Geeks work well together? Where do people act counter to the stereotype (it might be at work, it might be outside work. Either way it can be leverage). You can learn more in my book, *Start With What Works*.

7. **Clarify incentives.** Are you inadvertently rewarding the behaviours that feed into Suit v. Geek games and therefore drive Doom Loops?

8. **Coach both Suits and Geeks on their individual effectiveness.** Remember the light and dark sides of being a Suit or a Geek? Both groups have legitimate challenges (e.g., perfectionism and procrastination among Geeks, and bringing bad news and influencing across boundaries for Suits). There's no substitute for interactive help from the right kind of coaches.

9. **Make sure you're not enabling destructive behaviour.** For example, if you promote people who like to play stupid Suit v Geek games, you send a far more powerful signal than any workshop or speech at an all-hands meeting about stopping the games.

10. **Improve relationships by working together on substantive tasks rather than relying on workshops.** Workshops – unless you are very careful – always run the risk of being forgotten as soon as people get back to their inbox. Keep it real.

REVISITING THE REFLECTION QUESTIONS

I asked you these questions at the start of the book. In light of what you've read, have another look:

1. When you started out in your career, were you more interested in business or in technical matters?

2. How did you develop a wider perspective? Was it because of certain experiences, mentors, etc?

3. Who among your direct reports "gets it" and who is still tribal?

4. Who among other key managers and influencers, gets it and who is still tribal?

5. What could your business achieve if commercial people and technical people played better together?

6. What issues do Suits & Geeks problems cause the business? What would happen if that improved?

7. What have you tried?

8. What one change – if you were able to accomplish it – would represent a great return on investment?

9. What else would be possible once you achieved that one change?

LET'S TALK ABOUT TURNING YOUR COMMERCIAL AND TECHNICAL TALENT INTO A PROFIT POWERHOUSE

We know that business people and engineers can collaborate magnificently because the Growth Loops are what built the modern world. In your own career, you've probably also experienced the heady ride that comes from catching a Growth Loop.

If you're currently frustrated, it's perfectly understandable when you think how great your company can be.

I can help in a number of ways, but it always starts with a conversation.

Book a time below:

bassclusker.com/book-consult

ABOUT DR ANDY BASS

Other books by Andy

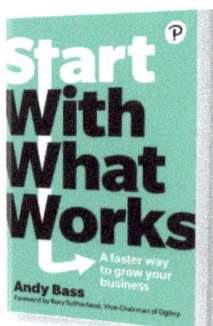

"A Geek who learned to wear a Suit", Andy started out studying computer science and ergonomics (human factors) at Aston University, researching "Good Old Fashioned AI" at BT Research Labs and then earning a PhD in software engineering back at Aston. After several years as a business school lecturer, he moved into consulting where he found his niche: bridging the contrasting worldviews of technical and commercial people to the concerns of senior executives in companies such as IAC Group, Rieke Packaging and Deutsche Bank.

Andy has described his approaches in four books and has also taught executives at the Oxford Saïd, Warwick and Aston Business Schools.

Outside work, Andy played lead guitar in a Rush tribute band, and honed his speaking skills dabbling in the dangerous world of stand-up comedy (with decidedly mixed results!).

Learn more at bassclusker.com

ACKNOWLEDGEMENTS

As with any book project, I owe many people thanks for their support and encouragement.

Debbie Jenkins, Joe Gregory, Louis Grenier, Mark Levy, Alan Weiss, Hanifa Shah, Maria Franzoni, Martin Worner, Ann Latham, Alastair Dryburgh, Tim Kist, Alex M H Smith, Sean Bacon, Katherine Lamb, Dian-Marie Hosking and my brother Stephen Bass all provided insightful critique and wise advice at various stages.

Ian Constance, David Pritchett, Jurga Žilinskienė, Paul Heldens, Damian O'Toole, Ninder Johal, Henry Chidgey, James Holland, Owen Maybank, Abbie Vlahakis, Jo Hodson, John Handley and Shanni Elcock shared their insights and perspectives on the "Games Suits and Geeks Play" across their various industries.

Thanks to Jenice Burke and G Sabini-Roberts for an outstanding job on branding and graphic design, and to Debbie Jenkins' team at Intellectual Perspectives Press for their hassle-free professionalism.

And most importantly, thanks and love to Barbara for her patience and unfailing support.